SEABISCUIT
VS WAR ADMIRAL

ANGEL BEA PUBLISHING

To Ash, Ali, Chrissy, Andrew, Kirby and Jo Jo—K.S.
For Aaron and Kat   —J.M.

Special thanks to Claudia Cornett, Todd Lyon and
Nancy Roe-Pimm for their expertise and support.
                                        —K.S. and J.M.

Publisher's Cataloging-in-Publication

Shehata, Kat.
    Seabiscuit vs. War Admiral : the greatest horse race in
history / by Kat Shehata ; illustrated by Jo McElwee.

    p. cm.
    SUMMARY : In 1938 two champion racehorses met.
Seabiscuit, the western underdog, and War Admiral, the high
spirited favorite, ran one-on-one in one of the most exciting
horse races in history.
    Audience : Ages 8 - 12.
    ISBN 0-9717843-1-0

    1. Horse racing- -United States- -Juvenile literature.
2. Seabiscuit (Race horse)- -Juvenile literature. 3. War
Admiral (Race horse)- - Juvenile literature. [1. Horse racing
---United States. 2. Seabiscuit (Race horse) 3. War Admiral
(Race horse)]
    1. McElwee, Jo. II. Title.

SF355.S4S44 2003   798.4
                          QB133-1088

Printed in China

PIMLICO SPECIAL
One mile and three sixteenths

Pimlico Racetrack
Baltimore, Maryland
November 1, 1938

GRANDSTAND

FINISH

1/4 MILE

1/2 MILE

NEXT RACE

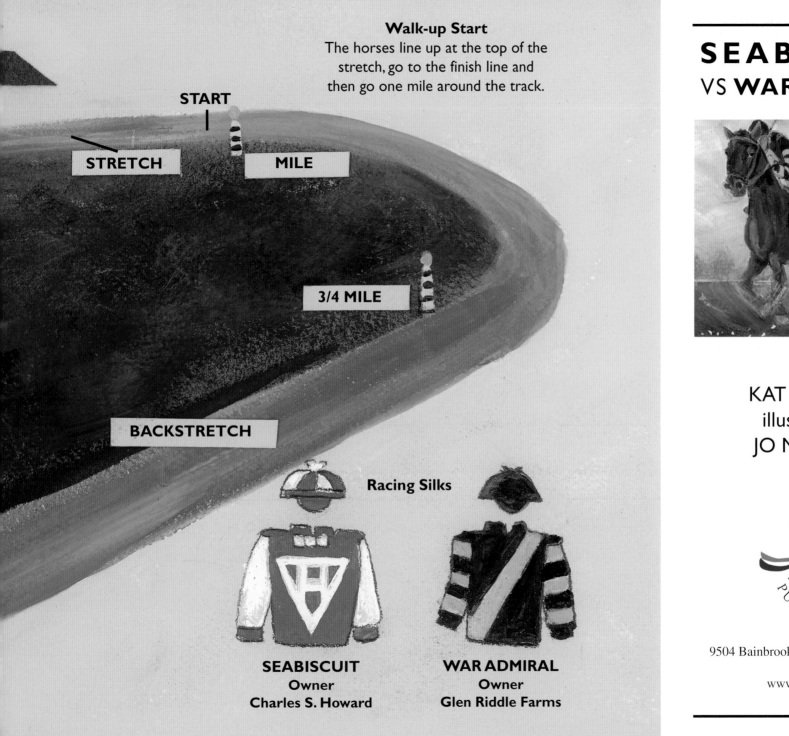

Walk-up Start
The horses line up at the top of the
stretch, go to the finish line and
then go one mile around the track.

START

STRETCH

MILE

3/4 MILE

BACKSTRETCH

Racing Silks

SEABISCUIT
Owner
Charles S. Howard

WAR ADMIRAL
Owner
Glen Riddle Farms

SEABISCUIT
VS WAR ADMIRAL

KAT SHEHATA
illustrated by
JO MCELWEE

ANGEL BEA
PUBLISHING

9504 Bainbrook • Cincinnati, Ohio 45249

www.angelbea.com

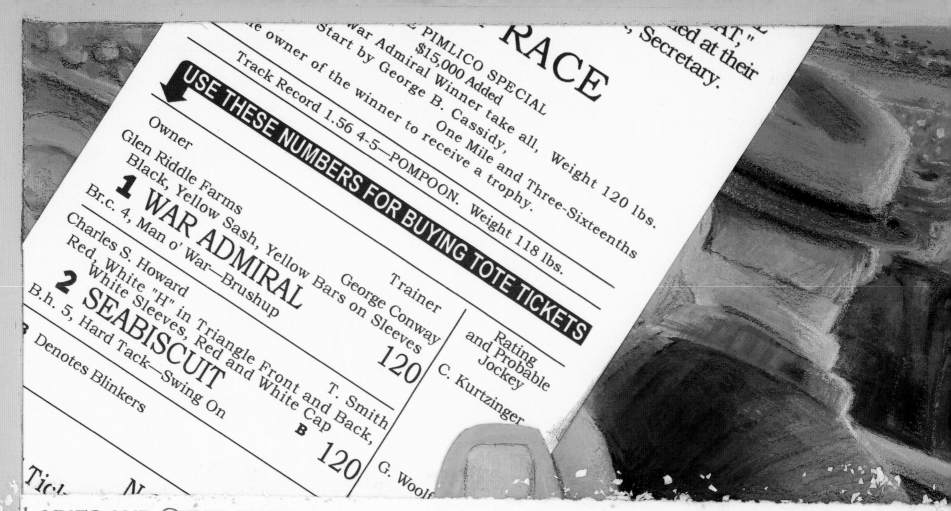

RACE

PIMLICO SPECIAL
$15,000 Added
War Admiral Winner take all, Weight 120 lbs.
Start by George B. Cassidy,
One Mile and Three-Sixteenths
The owner of the winner to receive a trophy. Weight 118 lbs.

Track Record 1.56 4-5—POMPOON. Weight 120 lbs.

USE THESE NUMBERS FOR BUYING TOTE TICKETS

Owner	Trainer	Rating and Probable Jockey
Glen Riddle Farms Black, Yellow Sash, Yellow Bars on Sleeves	George Conway	C. Kurtzinger
1 WAR ADMIRAL Br.c. 4, Man o' War—Brushup		120
Charles S. Howard Red, White "H" in Triangle Front and Back, White Sleeves, Red and White Cap	T. Smith	G. Woolf
2 SEABISCUIT B.h. 5, Hard Tack—Swing On	**B**	120

Denotes Blinkers

Tick   N

LADIES AND GENTLEMEN, IN A MOMENT, THE LONG AWAITED CLASSIC OF THE TURF.

On November 1, 1938, two legendary racehorses geared up for the most exciting horse race in history. Over 40,000 fans packed into Baltimore, Maryland's, Pimlico Race Course to witness Seabiscuit vs. War Admiral. Seabiscuit, the short, stocky underdog, and War Admiral, the high-spirited favorite, were winning races and breaking track records across the country. However, they had never raced against each other. The two champions were to meet at last at the Pimlico Special.

THE RACE BETWEEN WAR ADMIRAL AND SEABISCUIT WILL BE HELD ON THIS OVAL.

At that time in history, the country was on the verge of war and in a deep economic depression. The average salary was thirty-two dollars a week and the minimum wage was twenty-five cents an hour. Gambling was once again legal in the United States and race fans were anxious to bet their hard-earned money. Most people picked War Admiral to win over Seabiscuit. Why weren't people betting on Seabiscuit?

Seabiscuit was the son of a nasty-tempered **rogue** named Hard Tack and a gentle mare, named Swing On. Seabiscuit's father had great speed, but he was uncontrollable. Even Hall of Fame trainer "Sunny" Jim Fitzsimmons could not tame him. Seabiscuit's mother was the complete opposite of Hard Tack. She was a calm, gentle horse with thick knees and short legs. Swing On wasn't very fast though, so she never raced. When Seabiscuit was young, he seemed to take after his mother. His legs were stubby, his knees were thick and he looked "funny" when he ran. On the outside, Seabiscuit didn't look like a promising racehorse.

EQUAL WEIGHTS, 120 POUNDS. THE DISTANCE IS A MILE AND THREE SIXTEENTHS.

On the inside however, Seabiscuit had the heart of a champion. As Seabiscuit grew up he started to take on some of his father's characteristics. "Sunny" Jim worked with Seabiscuit and discovered he was a very fast runner, but had a bad "attitude" towards racing. Although he had great speed, he did not appear to enjoy the sport. In fact, he lost his first seventeen races. Seabiscuit was not living up to his potential with Fitzsimmons. He needed a change to jump-start his career. Since Seabiscuit didn't appear to be a winner, his owner, Samuel Riddle, sold him to another **barn** for the bargain price of $7,500.

IT'S A WALK UP START. EACH JOCKEY TRIED TO TAKE ADVANTAGE OF THE OTHER.

Seabiscuit's new team consisted of owner Charles Howard, jockey "Red" Pollard, and trainer "Silent" Tom Smith. Before Smith started training Seabiscuit, he wanted to get to know his personality. Smith learned that Seabiscuit loved to eat, he slept lying down, and he enjoyed the company of other animals. Seabiscuit would eat anything that was put in front of him. To keep his weight down, **grooms** were instructed to muzzle him at night to prevent him from eating his straw bedding. While most horses lock their legs and sleep standing, Seabiscuit preferred to bed down on a soft blanket of straw next to his stable mates: a dog, a spider monkey, and a **lead pony,** named Pumpkin.

THE STARTER CALLED THEM BACK..THEY ___ HAD THE CROWD ON THEIR TOES.

Seabiscuit enjoyed his new home and "family" very much. He became more gentle and appeared to develop a competitive spirit. Seabiscuit started to win races. Seabiscuit and his jockey, "Red" Pollard, made a great team. Together they were breaking track records and beating every horse that came along. Seabiscuit was the fastest horse in the West. In the East, however, there was another horse who was winning and breaking track records just like Seabiscuit. His name was War Admiral.

WAR ADMIRAL

1937 Horse of the Year

1st Kentucky Derby
1st Preakness Stakes
1st Belmont Stakes
1st Chesapeake Stakes
1st Pimlico Special
1st Washington Handicap

CHAMPION THREE YEAR OLD

YOU KNOW THIS REMINDS ME OF AN OLD QUARTER HORSE RACE IN THE WEST

War Admiral and Seabiscuit were blood related. They were the son and grandson of one of the greatest Thoroughbreds in history, Man o' War. Seabiscuit's father, Hard Tack, was War Admiral's brother. In 1937 War Admiral won every race he started and claimed the most prestigious prize in racing, the Triple Crown. He is one of only 11 champions in 100 years to earn a Triple Crown title. This prestigious honor is bestowed upon Thoroughbreds that win three major races in succession: The Kentucky Derby, Preakness Stakes, and Belmont Stakes. War Admiral's victory at Belmont was bittersweet. An injury prevented him from racing again for several months.

COWBOYS AND INDIANS. WHAT THEY CALL AN ASK AND ANSWER START

War Admiral's injury at Belmont happened straight out of the gate. War Admiral sprinted to the lead the way he always did. This time, however, he was running so fast his front and rear hooves grabbed, ripping a chunk out of his forefoot. This injury must have been painful, but War Admiral did not stop racing. He ran spraying blood across the track all the way to the finish line. It wasn't until he reached the winners circle that Charley Kurtsinger, his jockey, noticed the injury. War Admiral not only won the race, but he beat Man o' War's speed record as well. In 1937 War Admiral was named Horse of the Year.

NOW THEY'RE TURNING ONCE MORE, WALKING BACK THERE TOGETHER SIDE BY SIDE.

War Admiral was a natural competitor. The lively activity of race day seemed to fill him with nervous excitement. He was so competitive it was difficult for handlers to hold him back when the saddling bell rang. His temperament was fiery and skittish, like his brother Hard Tack, yet his personality usually worked to his advantage. He chomped at the **bit** all the way to the post and would rear up, shaking off starters. He never willingly walked into the **gate**. Once the starters got him in he would act up causing delays and **false starts**.

EITHER HORSE IS LIABLE TO KICK. GET THOSE HORSES FURTHER APART YOU JOCKEYS.

War Admiral was the best horse in the East and Seabiscuit was the best horse in the West. Race fans were anxious for the two champions to meet. The horses' owners decided to make the dream a reality. They agreed to arrange a one-on-one horse race, called a match race. Because of War Admiral's bad behavior at the starting gate his owner, Samuel Riddle, insisted the race begin with no gate, or a walk-up start. Howard agreed to begin the race with a starting bell. He had one condition, too. The track had to be "**fast**," or dry. Seabiscuit did not run well in the mud. If the track was too wet because of rain, the race would be called off.

SEABISCUIT HAD ABOUT A LENGTH THE BEST OF IT. KURTSINGER WOULDN'T TAKE IT.

War Admiral appeared to have the advantage over Seabiscuit in this race. First of all, a severe injury prevented Pollard from racing. Seabiscuit needed a new jockey. Secondly, up until that time, every match race in history had been won by the horse that was in the lead from the start. In 1937 War Admiral never let a single horse in front of him. Seabiscuit was a come-from-behind winner. He took it slow in the beginning until he got the signal from his jockey. Once the whip cracked he ran down his opponents in the homestretch. Each horse had his own style that worked for him. Did the trainers and jockeys change their strategy for this particular race?

Now, LOOKOUT, LOOKOUT. THEY'RE READY AGAIN. NEITHER JOCKEY IS

On the day of the race the sun came out. The race was on! Charley Kurtsinger, wearing black and yellow silks, had the leg up on War Admiral and George Woolf, with red and white silks, was riding Seabiscuit. The Admiral prepared himself for the race the way he always did, rearing up and tormenting his handlers. Seabiscuit calmly walked away from Pumpkin and his owners and headed for the post. The officials were ready to begin the race, but at the last minute the starter discovered the track's bell was broken. With no other options, he asked Smith if he could use his homemade bell.

HE SHOT WAR ADMIRAL RIGHT BEHIND SEABISCUIT TO THE OUTSIDE FENCE

War Admiral's trainer, George Conway, and jockey Charley Kurtsinger were confident their horse was faster than Seabiscuit. Therefore, Conway concentrated on building War Admiral's stamina to endure the long distance. Smith was preparing Seabiscuit and his new jockey, George "The Iceman" Woolf, too. He put together a homemade bell that sounded like the starting bell at Pimlico. When Smith rang the bell Woolf cracked the whip on Seabiscuit's backside. This taught Seabiscuit to run as fast as he could right out of the gate. The day before the match, Woolf examined the track. It was muddy, or slow, because of heavy rains. Seabiscuit could only run his best on a hard surface. Woolf noticed that an imprint from a tractor left a hard dry path around the track. He memorized the trail.

WILLING TO TAKE ONE INCH THE WORST OF IT. AHH. AND THEY'RE OFF!

The flag was raised and the horses lined up. War Admiral was positioned next to the rail and Seabiscuit was in the number 2 **post position**. Just as the starter was about to ring the bell, Woolf pulled Seabiscuit back. He wanted to make War Admiral nervous. Then, the horses lined up again. This time Kurtsinger pulled War Admiral back. The jockeys trotted their horses around and lined up once again. Clem McCarthy, the radio sportscaster, described this delay when one jockey pulls out and then the other as an "ask and answer" start.

SEABISCUIT IS COMING TO ME, ONE LENGTH, TWO LENGTHS IN THE LEAD.

On the third try, Seabiscuit and War Admiral were lined up at exactly the same moment. The starter rang the bell and they were off. The two Thoroughbreds pounded down the track neck and neck. It was widely anticipated that War Admiral would take the early lead. The crowd went wild with excitement as Woolf cracked the whip and Seabiscuit edged in front of War Admiral. Kurtsinger and War Admiral were not accustomed to being outrun. The answer to the question that every trainer, reporter, and fan wanted to know was finally clear. Seabiscuit was faster than War Admiral. The question that remained to be seen was, "Could Seabiscuit keep up the pace to outrun 1937's Horse of the Year"?

WAR ADMIRAL RIGHT ON HIS HEELS. KURTSINGER SITTING STILL AND BIDING HIS TIME.

Around the first turn Seabiscuit was still ahead. Woolf went left and took the rail from Kurtsinger. Then he slowed Seabiscuit down right in front of War Admiral. This allowed Seabiscuit to conserve energy and forced Kurtsinger to make a decision to either slow down or pass. War Admiral was getting closer and closer to Seabiscuit. Woolf held the reins tight and Seabiscuit had the lead by a **length** and a half. Around they went and Seabiscuit was still in front. The fans in the **infield** leaned against the inner rail to get a better look. The fence began to bend.

THEY'RE HALFWAY DOWN THE BACKSTRETCH AND THERE GOES WAR ADMIRAL.

Kurtsinger was surprised by 'Biscuit's speed. He had to change his strategy. Instead of exhausting War Admiral to keep up, he would let Woolf wear out Seabiscuit. Kurtsinger must have thought Seabiscuit would get tired and slow down. He might have been right, *if* Seabiscuit had been running at top speed. Going into the **backstretch** Seabiscuit was still leading by a length and half, then two lengths. Then, Kurtsinger cracked the whip.

AND IT'S EITHER ONE. TAKE YOUR CHOICE. AND THEY'RE HEAD AND HEAD.

In just a few strides War Admiral was even with Seabiscuit. The crowd cheered! The horses were **neck and neck**. Then War Admiral took the lead. Then, Seabiscuit sped up. He got in front of War Admiral again! Just ahead, the inner fence that separated the people from the track had fallen down. Excited fans leaned against the rail waiting for the horses to race towards the **stretch**.

Turning into the stretch, War Admiral was close behind Seabiscuit. "Sunny" Jim Fitzsimmons, Seabiscuit's first trainer, clutched his "Seabiscuit to win" ticket as the horses flew around the track. In Boston, "Red" Pollard listened to the race while lying in a hospital bed. In Washington, D.C., President Roosevelt listened on his radio at the White House. Forty million more fans, many of whom had never cared about horse racing before, listened to the race on their radios at home.

IT'S THE BEST HORSE NOW. IT'S HORSE AGAINST HORSE. BOTH OF THEM DRIVING

Around the far turn Seabiscuit and War Admiral were headed for home. They were coupled shoulder to shoulder, head to head, eye to eye. Woolf was running Seabiscuit on the hard surface of the tire track. At this point the game between trainers and jockeys had been played. Tom Smith's **schooling**, Conway's endurance training, Woolf's cunning, and Kurtsinger's **driving** got the horses where they were. Now it was horse against horse.

WOOLF HAS PUT AWAY HIS WHIP. IT'S SEABISCUIT BY THREE. SEABISCUIT BY THREE

Around the turn as they headed for home Woolf cracked the whip, asking Seabiscuit for every-thing he had. "The Iceman" loosened the reins and 'Biscuit answered. He dropped his chin, laid his ears back and raced towards the finish line. War Admiral was trailing as Seabiscuit broke away by one length, two lengths, three lengths…then the race was won.

SEABISCUIT IS THE WINNER. AND YOU NEVER SAW SUCH A WILD CROWD.

Seabiscuit breezed over the finish line leaving War Admiral in his dust. "Seabiscuit by four!" sportscaster Clem McCarthy yelled wildly. As Seabiscuit slowed to a gallop, thousands of fans burst through the infield chasing their underdog hero. In the winners circle Seabiscuit was donned with a blanket of yellow flowers. War Admiral's barn met their defeated champion, and slipped away almost unnoticed.

SEABISCUIT WINS BY FOUR LENGTHS. SEABISCUIT IS THE WINNER FROM END TO END

Smith and Howard greeted their champions in the winners circle. Caught up in the excitement, Smith ripped apart the bouquet of flowers and tossed souvenirs to the fans. But before the blanket was gone, Seabiscuit plucked a single flower from his chest and savored his victory. Seabiscuit, the champion underdog, was named Horse of the Year in 1938.

HORSE RACING TERMS

Backstretch: stable area; long, straight part of the track on the far side of the grandstand

Barn: owner, trainer, and caretakers of a particular horse

Bay: dark brown horse with a black mane and tail

Bit: metal bar across the horse's mouth to which the reins are attached

Bolt: to run off unexpectedly

Broodmare: a female horse used for breeding

Bug boy: apprentice jockey

Claiming race: race that features horses for sale

Clockers: people who time workouts

Conditioned: trained

Connections: owner, trainer, and other handlers of a horse

Dam: a horse's mother

Dark horse: a horse having long odds but a good chance of winning

Driving: an all out urging by the jockey

Early foot: good speed at the beginning of a race

Exerciser: person who rides a horse in training workouts

False start: when a horse starts the race before the starter gives the signal

Fast: the normal condition of the racing surface; i.e., not wet or muddy from rain

Flank: rear belly area behind ribs

Foal: a newborn horse

Front runner: horses that prefer to run in front of other horses

Furlong: one-eighth of a mile; 220 yards; 660 feet. (approx. 200 meters)

Gait: ways a horse can move by lifting its feet in a particular rhythm

Gate: a boxed in area where horses line up before a race

Game: competitive

Get: the offspring of a stallion

Going away: winning while drawing away from the others

Groom: person who takes care of horses

Hand: unit of length equal to 4 inches or 10.16 centimeters

Handicapping: to predict the outcome of a race

Hardboot: an old-time horseman

Homestretch: the end of the final turn closest to the finish line

Infield: the area on the inner circumference of the track

Impost: weights added under a horse's saddle to weaken its advantage over the field

Leads: person who walks a horse, particularly to the post position

Lead pony: any work horse at the track; the horse that leads a race horse to the post

Length: approximately eight to ten feet

Maiden: a horse (male or female) that has never won a race

Match race: a winner-take-all race between two horses

Mount: horse assigned to a jockey

Mudder: a horse that performs well in the mud

Neck and neck: horses that are even during a race

Odds: likelihood that one competitor will win over another

On the nose: a bet to win

Paddock: saddling enclosure

Post: the starting gate

Post position: starting position assigned to a horse before the race

Pull up: to stop a horse or slow it down during a race or immediately afterwards

Purse: money winnings

Reducing: losing weight by dieting or sweating off water weight

Rein out: to pull up on the reins in an effort to stop, slow down, or rear up a horse

Rogue: horse that can not be broken of bad habits

School: to train a horse, notably at the starting gate and at the paddock

Short: lack of fitness whereby a horse tires in the stretch

Silks: colorful jackets, representing the owners' team colors, worn by jockeys

Sire: a horse's father

Slow: when a track is wet or muddy because of rain

Spit the bit: when an exhausted horse backs up and will not persevere any longer

Stallion: a male horse used in breeding

Starter: racing official who starts a race

Stake: the commission paid to the winning jockey, trainer, or groom

Stewards: the three officially appointed judges of equine and human conduct at the racetrack; the official judges of race and riding inquiries

Stick: whip

Stud: male horse; stallion

Tight: a fit and ready horse

Thoroughbred: a breed of horses that can be traced back over 300 years to three foundation sires: the Darley Arabian, the Godolphin Arabian, and the Byerly Turk. These stallions were brought to England from the Middle East and bred to English mares. The result of selective breeding produced horses that could carry weight while running at top speed.

Ticks: seconds

Under wraps: a horse that has not been allowed to do its best, usually due to the trainer's instructions or the jockey's judgment

Used up: a horse that has become prematurely exhausted

Weanling: age description of horse from birth to one year of age

Wire: finish line

NTRA Charities

The goal of NTRA Charities is to help horses and people.

NTRA Charities works with Thoroughbred racing organizations like ReRun, Tranquility Farm, and the Thoroughbred Retirement Foundation. These organizations help find new homes for racehorses after they retire from racing. NTRA Charities also helps promote the Grayson-Jockey Club Research Foundation, which funds medical research to keep horses healthy and safe.

The people of racing get help from NTRA Charities' affiliates, too. Organizations like The Jockey Club Foundation, the Race Track Chaplaincy of America, and Thoroughbred Charities of America help meet the needs of people who work at racetracks or on horse farms.

NTRA Charities also helps promote Ronald McDonald House Charities. This charity provides the comforts of home to families of sick children staying at nearby hospitals. There are more than 200 Ronald McDonald Houses in 33 countries around the world.

For more information on NTRA Charities and the organizations it supports, visit the National Thoroughbred Racing Association Web site, www.NTRA.com.

NTRA Charities is a nonprofit, 501(c)(3) subsidiary of the National Thoroughbred Racing Association.